Emotional Self-Awareness

CAUSES & EFFECTS OF EMOTIONS

Embarrassment, Shame, and Guilt

Happiness

Fear and Anxiety

Romantic Attraction

Anger

Optimism and Self-Confidence

Stress and Tension

Sadness

Empathy and Compassion

Envy and Jealousy

Surprise and Flexibility

Emotional Self-Awareness

Loneliness

CAUSES & EFFECTS OF EMOTIONS

Emotional Self-Awareness

Rosa Waters

Mason Crest

Mason Crest
450 Parkway Drive, Suite D
Broomall, PA 19008
www.masoncrest.com

Printed and bound in the United States of America.

First printing
9 8 7 6 5 4 3 2 1

Series ISBN: 978-1-4222-3067-1
ISBN: 978-1-4222-3070-1
ebook ISBN: 978-1-4222-8763-7

The Library of Congress has cataloged the
hardcopy format(s) as follows:
          Library of Congress Cataloging-in-Publication Data

Waters, Rosa, 1957-
  Emotional self-awareness / Rosa Waters.
      pages cm. — (Causes & effects of emotions)
  Includes index.
  Audience: Age 12+
  Audience: Grade 7 to 8.
      ISBN 978-1-4222-3070-1 (hardback) — ISBN 978-1-4222-3067-1
(series) — ISBN 978-1-4222-8763-7 (ebook) 1. Emotions in adolescence—
Juvenile literature. 2. Emotions in children—Juvenile literature I. Title.
  BF724.3.E5W38 2015
  152.4—dc23
                                                      2014004379

CONTENTS

Introduction   6

1. What Are Emotions?   9

2. How Are Emotions Connected
   to Your Brain & Body?   21

3. How Do Emotions Change Your Life?   33

4. Understanding Your Emotions   43

Find Out More   60

Series Glossary of Key Terms   61

Index   62

Picture Credits   63

About the Author & Consultant   64

KEY ICONS TO LOOK FOR:

 Text-Dependent Questions: These questions send the reader back to the text for more careful attention to the evidence presented there.

 Words to Understand: These words with their easy-to-understand definitions will increase the reader's understanding of the text, while building vocabulary skills.

 Series Glossary of Key Terms: This back-of-the book glossary contains terminology used throughout this series. Words found here increase the reader's ability to read and comprehend higher-level books and articles in this field.

 Research Projects: Readers are pointed toward areas of further inquiry connected to each chapter. Suggestions are provided for projects that encourage deeper research and analysis.

 Sidebars: This boxed material within the main text allows readers to build knowledge, gain insights, explore possibilities, and broaden their perspectives by weaving together additional information to provide realistic and holistic perspectives.

INTRODUCTION

The journey of self-discovery for young adults can be a passage that includes times of introspection as well joyful experiences. It can also be a complicated route filled with confusing road signs and hazards along the way. The choices teens make will have lifelong impacts. From early romantic relationships to complex feelings of anxiousness, loneliness, and compassion, this series of books is designed specifically for young adults, tackling many of the challenges facing them as they navigate the social and emotional world around and within them. Each chapter explores the social emotional pitfalls and triumphs of young adults, using stories in which readers will see themselves reflected.

Adolescents encounter compound issues today in home, school, and community. Many young adults may feel ill equipped to identify and manage the broad range of emotions they experience as their minds and bodies change and grow. They face many adult problems without the knowledge and tools needed to find satisfactory solutions. Where do they fit in? Why are they afraid? Do others feel as lonely and lost as they do? How do they handle the emotions that can engulf them when a friend betrays them or they fail to make the grade? These are all important questions that young adults may face. Young adults need guidance to pilot their way through changing feelings that are influenced by peers, family relationships, and an ever-changing world. They need to know that they share common strengths and pressures with their peers. Realizing they are not alone with their questions can help them develop important attributes of resilience and hope.

The books in this series skillfully capture young people's everyday, real-life emotional journeys and provides practical and meaningful information that can offer hope to all who read them.

It covers topics that teens may be hesitant to discuss with others, giving them a context for their own feelings and relationships. It is an essential tool to help young adults understand themselves and their place in the world around them—and a valuable asset for teachers and counselors working to help young people become healthy, confident, and compassionate members of our society.

Cindy Croft, M.A.Ed
Director of the Center for Inclusive Child Care at Concordia University

Words to Understand

spectrum: A wide range of something, stretching from one extreme to the other.

philosophers: People who think deeply about ethics, the mind, the universe, or the meaning of life.

empathy: The ability to understand and share in others' feelings.

evolutionary: Having to do with the process by which organisms change and develop over many generations.

species: A certain kind of organism that can produce offspring with others of the same kind.

genetic: Having to do with DNA, the code inside our cells that determines what characteristics we have.

psychologists: Experts who study the human mind and emotions.

cognitive: Having to do with knowledge and thought.

appraisal: The act of evaluating or assessing someone or something.

theory: A suggested explanation for something, supported by scientific evidence.

neurologists: Doctors or scientists who study the brain and nerves.

optimism: A feeling of hope or confidence in the future.

ONE

WHAT ARE EMOTIONS?

You get up in the morning and look out the window. The sun is shining and you remember that today you're going to see your girlfriend. The thought makes you smile, and you find yourself humming as you take your shower and get ready for school.

When you go downstairs to eat breakfast, though, you discover that your little brother has drank the last of the orange juice and the milk, so there's only water to drink with your toast. Your good mood fades. "Why did you let him drink it *all*?" you snap at your mother.

Your brother and you pile in the car for the drive to school. You're still feeling annoyed with both your brother and your mother, so you look out the window and don't join in their conversation. Suddenly, your mother slams on the breaks. "What the—!" you shout.

EMOTIONAL SELF-AWARENESS

You have many emotions every day!

Make Connections

- Experts say that people feel only 6 main emotions— happiness, surprise, fear, sadness, disgust, and anger—and that all the other emotions we experience are some sort of combination or variation of these.
- There are more than 600 words in the English language used to describe emotions.
- We use 42 muscles in our faces to express emotions.

A truck has pulled out in front of you, and now your mother is struggling to control the car as she swerves to keep from running into the back of the truck. The car ends up on the side of the road in the ditch. Luckily, no one is hurt. Your heart is pounding and you realize you are shaking all over.

In the space of an hour, you've felt three emotions: happiness, anger, and fear. Before the day is over, you may feel a whole *spectrum* of other emotions, from sadness to embarrassment, surprise to disappointment.

INSIDE FEELINGS AND OUTSIDE REALITY

Our emotions are the feelings inside our minds that come and go. We've been experiencing them our entire life, ever since we were babies. Sometimes we feel happy, and sometimes we feel sad; sometime we feel angry, sometimes we're scared, and sometimes we are bored. All these feelings come and go inside us. We may feel as though we have little control over them.

We may also feel as though our inside feelings are telling us about outside reality. So when we feel sad, for example, we may believe that the world really is a gloomy place where bad things happen. We believe our sadness tells us something about the

EMOTIONAL SELF-AWARENESS

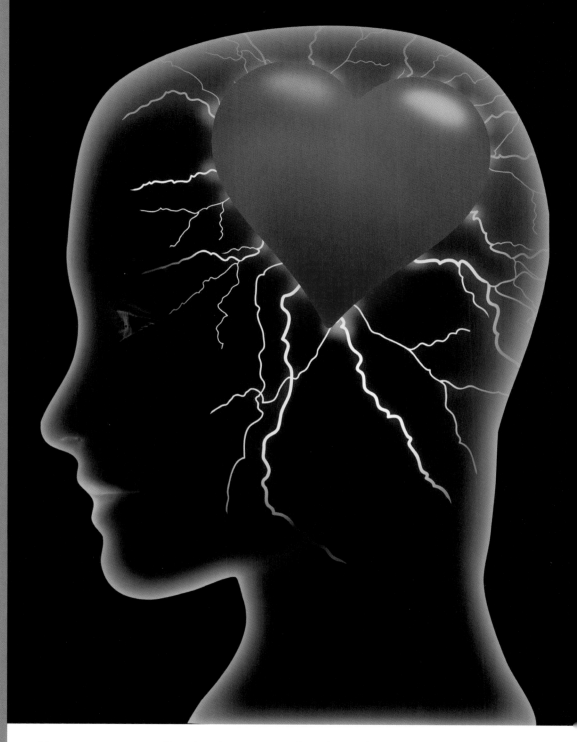

Your emotions actually take place in your head, not the beating organ in your chest.

outside the world. Really, though, our sadness only tells us about ourselves and how we are responding to the outside world.

CHANGING IDEAS

Philosophers used to think that emotions were the feelings of the soul—or the heart—while physical pain and other sensations were the feelings of the body. Psychologists and scientists today know that emotions actually take place in our bodies, especially in our brains, but a lot of us still tend to think of these feelings as though they're taking place in a different sort of reality from either our bodies or the outside world. We often speak of emotional health as though it's something separate from physical health. We still talk about the "heart" as the place where our emotions live. None of us think that the beating organ in our chests is really what makes us happy or sad, angry or amused—and yet we say things like:

"My heart broke." (When we mean, "I feel sad.")
"My heart leapt." ("I was suddenly happy.")
"You'll be in my heart forever." ("I'll always love you.)
"He has a heart of stone." ("He lacks **empathy** for others.")
"She's soft-hearted." ("She has a lot of empathy.")
"My heart was heavy." ("I was sad.")
"Eat your heart out!" ("Wish for something you'll never get!")
"I poured out my heart to her." ("I expressed my feelings to her in words.")
"I believe it from the bottom of my heart." ("I am emotionally committed to this belief.")
"My heart is set on going." ("I feel stubborn about my decision to go.")
"I had a change of heart." ("I feel differently about something from what I did before.")

When we use these figures of speech, we don't stop to think what we're saying. We know what we *mean*. But phrases like

Charles Darwin.

Charles Darwin changed the way we think about many things when he brought his ideas about evolution to the world.

these show that we still are thinking of our emotions as coming from some mysterious place inside us—not from the heart that beats blood but from the "heart" that is very close to our soul, that deepest part of our identities, the part of us that *feels*.

In the past hundred years or so, though, scientists have come to think about emotions quite differently. Toward the end of the nineteenth century, Charles Darwin published an article called "The Expression of the Emotions in Man and Animals." In this paper, Darwin expressed his belief that emotions serve an important *evolutionary* purpose. In order for a *species* to continue, Darwin said, it needs to survive and pass on its *genetic* information to the next generation. Emotions like fear served to protect humans from danger, so the humans who experienced it survived to pass on their genes—and included in this genetic information was the ability to feel fear. Emotions like love gave humans the desire to reproduce and have babies, so humans who experienced it also passed along their genes.

At the most basic level, according to Darwin and the scientists who came after him, emotions are what happen when our brains look at something outside us—say a large animal that's about to attack us or a pretty girl who is smiling at us—and interprets whatever is going on in terms of survival. Then our brains react in the way that will best help us to survive and reproduce. Emotions are the way our brains convince us we should act in a certain way to achieve those two most basic goals, survival and reproduction.

Based on this thinking, *psychologists* in the twentieth century formed two main ideas about emotions. According to the first of these, the "*cognitive appraisal theory*," emotions are judgments you pass about how much the current situation meets your goals. So you would feel happiness when your goals are being satisfied—for example, when you know you're going to see your girlfriend—but you might feel anger when your goals are blocked—such as when you want to drink milk with your breakfast and discover that your brother hasn't left you any. Other psychologists and scientists, however, argued that emotions are merely changes

Ex: 3382
Se: 4
Im: 12
OSag L6.5

HOSPITAL
F 58 380180
Aug 31 03
08:43:51 AM
Mag = 1.0
FL: 000
ROT: 000

SE
TR:3
TE:9
EC:1

An MRI allows scientists to look inside the brain and see what's going on there.

Make Connections

Magnetic resonance imaging (MRI) is a test that uses a magnetic field and pulses of radio wave energy to take pictures of organs and structures inside the body. For an MRI test, the area of the body being studied is placed inside a special machine that contains a strong magnet. Pictures from an MRI scan are digital images that can be saved and stored on a computer for more study.

in our bodies, such as heart rate, breathing rate, perspiration, and hormone levels.

Many psychologists didn't feel that either explanation was quite good enough to explain the full range of emotions that humans experience. The irritation you feel when your brother drinks all the orange juice is quite different from the anger you might feel if you found out a friend had talked about you behind your back—and both are different from the outrage you might experience if you heard on the news that a group of people was being treated cruelly and unfairly. And yet all three emotional states have something to do with anger, and they all trigger similar reactions in your body.

Psychologists and *neurologists* think that the finely tuned spectrum of emotions that most humans experience has to do with the fact that the brain is a very complicated machine, capable of combining many processes all at once. Different parts of the brain do different things. Some parts interpret the messages brought in from our physical senses, other parts make judgments, others respond to body changes, and still others send out messages about how to act next. When all these parts work together, they create a wide range of different emotions.

Scientists are doing lots of research on human emotions. They've done experiments on brain cells. They've used machines

Research Project

Find out more about Charles Darwin's theory of evolution. Use the Internet and the library to research Darwin's theories and how they changed the way we look at the world. Discuss at least one other way of thinking that Darwin's theories challenged.

like MRIs to actually look inside people's brains and see what's going on in there. But with all their research, emotions are still mysterious.

POINTING TO WHAT'S IMPORTANT

One thing that most experts agree on is that emotions serve an important function in our lives. They direct our attention toward things that are important. When something makes us happy, for example, our brains say, "Notice this! Try to get more of this in your life!" Or when something scares us, the reaction in our brains tells us, "Be careful!"

When we were young children, all of us learned from our emotions. We learned what made us happy and what made us sad, what scared us and what made us laugh. We learned to change our behavior in response. Positive emotions—like joy and excitement and *optimism*—give us the energy we needed to be creative and do amazing things. Negative feelings—like grief and anger and fear—aren't all bad either. They can also serve important functions in our lives. They teach us to stay way from things that might hurt us.

Text-Dependent Questions

1. What are the six main emotions experts say people feel?

2. Explain how people used to think about emotions and compare it to what scientists think today.

3. Describe what Charles Darwin believed about emotions.

4. How does the cognitive appraisal theory explain emotions?

5. Explain how emotions help us to identify what is important in our lives.

We still have a lot to learn about our emotions. Scientists are exploring the connections between our emotions, our brains, and the rest of our bodies. They're making important discoveries that help us all understand emotions a little better.

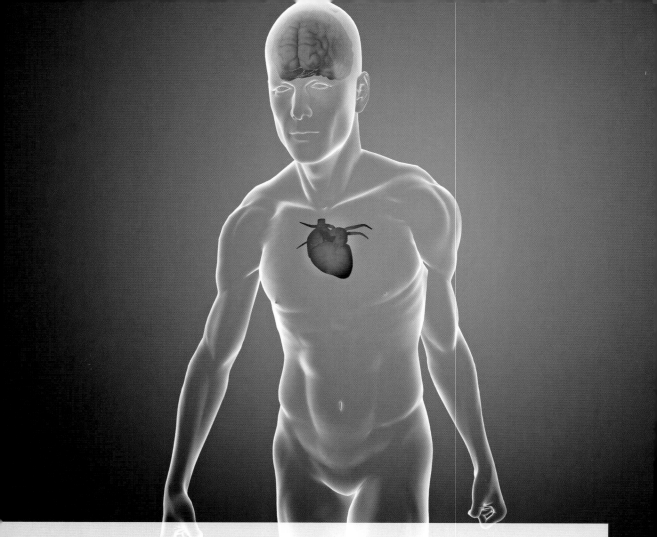

Words to Understand

pessimistic: Expecting bad things to happen.

regenerate: Grow back or heal.

researchers: Scientists who try to make new discoveries by doing experiments and collecting data.

stimuli: Things that cause reactions.

neuroscientists: Scientists who study the brain and nerves.

receptors: The parts of a cell that receive chemical messages.

rational: Based on logic, instead of impulse or emotion.

TWO

HOW ARE EMOTIONS CONNECTED TO YOUR BRAIN & BODY?

Even though scientists can look inside people's brains now using MRIs, it's still hard to say exactly what's going on in there. Everyone experiences emotions, but scientists do not all agree on what emotions are or how they should be measured or studied. Emotions are still hard to understand or predict.

Say you woke up with a headache and you feel like you're getting a head cold. This time, when you see the sun is shining outside your window and you remember you're going to see your girlfriend soon, you feel a faint flicker of happiness—but you're so miserable that the happiness fades away into a sense of discouragement. You remember that your girlfriend and you had a fight recently, and you wonder if she's thinking about breaking up with you. You shower and get dressed, but you're feeling sad and *pessimistic* about the day ahead. When you go downstairs to eat breakfast, you discover that your brother has drank all the milk

Your brain's reactions will change based on the things that you experience.

Your emotions may change from happiness to fear, from sadness to anger, all in the blink of an eye.

and orange juice, but you don't really care; you're not hungry, and all you want is a cup of hot tea. Your mother makes you the tea, and you feel a surge of love for her. Then in the car, you try to distract yourself from your dreary feelings by talking with your mother and your brother. You see the truck about ready to cut off your mother, and you shout, "Watch out!" Thanks to your warning, your mother pulls smoothly into the other lane and navigates safely around the truck. "Wow," she says to you, her voice shaking a little, "if it wasn't for you, I think we would have just had an accident." Your heart is pounding hard, but you feel a warm sense of pride, and you give your mother a grin. You realize it's not such a bad day after all.

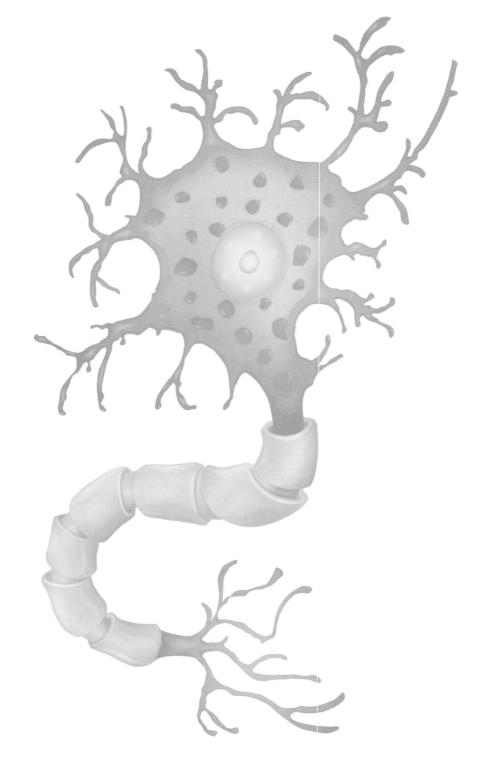

Your brain is a network of cells like this, all constantly sending messages between each other.

Make Connections

Because neurotransmitters have such an impact on our emotions, if they're out of balance we may find ourselves responding more negatively to life than we might otherwise. This could make us feel sad all the time—what psychologists call depression—or worried all the time—what psychologists call an anxiety disorder. Scientists have developed medications that make the brain produce more of certain brain chemicals that affect mood. Antidepressants change how the brain produces serotonin, which makes people generally feel happier. Anti-anxiety medications tweak how the brain produces norepinephrine. Taking medicines like these isn't meant to take away the range of emotions a person experiences—so a person taking an antidepressant, for example, won't feel happy all the time. Instead, these medications are intended to get the brain back in balance, so it can function normally.

Same day, just a little different because you woke up with a head cold! The messages your body passed to your brain were just slightly different—and so your brain responded a bit differently as well.

There's a lot going on in your brain whenever you feel an emotion. Emotions aren't only feelings triggered by outside events. They also involve how we process and respond to those feelings. So a lot of factors can shape any emotion. And because the brain is so complicated, emotions are very complex. Your brain's cells and its various structures work together at different levels to create the feelings we call emotions.

BRAIN CHEMICALS

Your brain is a network of neurons (brain cells) that processes vast quantities of information every second. Neurons pass messages

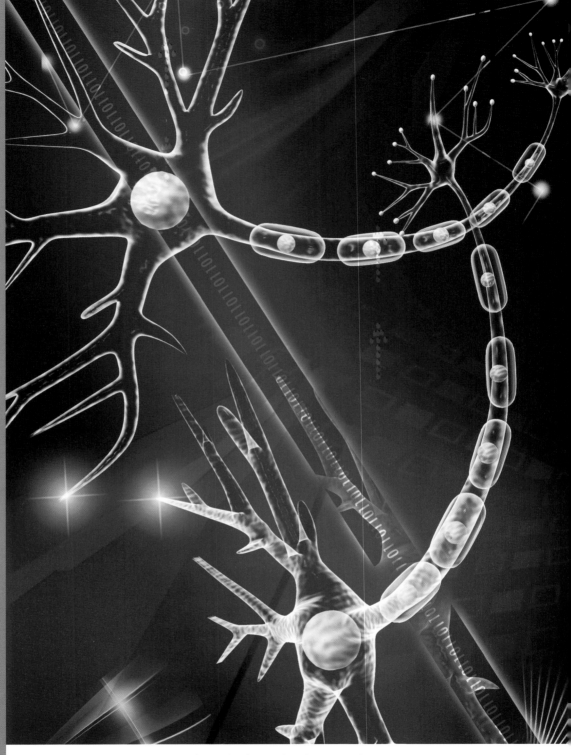

Neurons never quite touch—which is why they need neurotransmitters to carry the messages across the tiny gaps between them.

Research Project

Create a map of the brain. Using a picture of a brain from the Internet or a book, draw it on a piece of poster board. Outline the parts of the brain described in this chapter, color them different colors from each other, and label them. Find at least three other brain parts and label them on your brain map as well. Describe what each brain part does, including the parts you included that weren't discussed in this chapter.

from one cell to another. Picture a whole string of football players, passing a football between them, and you have a very rough picture of how neurons work. They use chemicals called neurotransmitters to carry the message—the "football"—across the tiny gaps between each cell. These chemicals allow all the parts of the brain to communicate with each other.

Three of the most important neurotransmitters are dopamine, serotonin, and norepinephrine. Dopamine is connected to good feelings. Certain behaviors cause your brain to reward you with a burst of dopamine, giving you a happy feeling of pleasure. This teaches your brain to want to do that particular behavior again and again. Serotonin is the neurotransmitter that has to do with memory and learning. Scientists believe it also plays a part in helping brain cells **regenerate**, and it's been linked to easing depression. If you don't have enough serotonin, you may feel an increase in anger, anxiety, depression, and scared feelings. Norepinephrine helps you control stress and anxiety.

EMOTIONAL SELF-AWARENESS

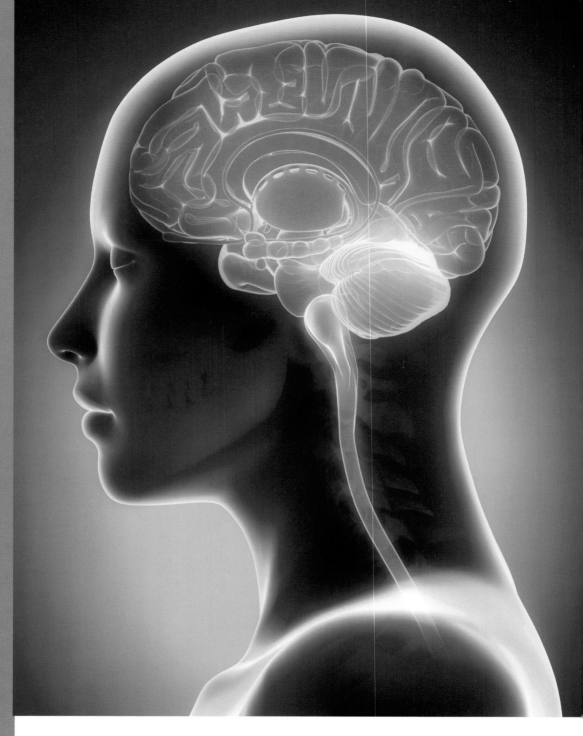

Inside your brain are various structures that play different roles in your emotional life.

DIFFERENT BRAIN STRUCTURES, DIFFERENT EMOTIONS

Researchers believe that different parts of the brain are most involved with emotions. The main part of the brain responsible for processing emotions is called the limbic system. Within it are the brain's frontal lobes and the amygdala, where a lot of emotions take place. Feelings of happiness and pleasure are linked to the prefrontal cortex (the part of the brain that's sometimes known as "gray matter"). Anger, fear, sadness, and other negative emotions are linked to the amygdala.

The amygdala is an almond-shaped mass of gray matter inside your limbic system. It's what takes a look at outside *stimuli* and decides whether something dangerous is going on. It's the source of what's called the "fight-or-flight response." When you almost had the accident on your way to school, the amygdala took a look at the truck in front of you and shouted, "Danger! Watch out!" It sent out messages to the rest of your body, telling it to get ready for danger.

When this response was evolving, thousands of years ago, most dangers humans faced were things that either had to be fought or run away from. If your great-great-many-many-times-great-grandfather was facing a charging woolly mammoth, for example, he had to either attack it and kill it—or run away from it as fast as he could. As a result, his heart beat harder and he breathed faster, sending more oxygen to his muscles. His amygdala got his body ready. In today's world, danger is often not quite as simple—but the amygdala doesn't know that. It still gets our bodies ready for fight or flight, the same way it's been doing for thousands and thousands of years.

The hypothalamus is another brain structure that plays a role in emotions. It sits at the mid-line of the brain and extends to the base of the brain. It's not much larger than the tip of your little finger, but its job is so important that sometimes *neuroscientists* call it "the brain within the brain." When your amygdala shouts

Make Connections

Roller coasters, scary movies, and haunted houses are all examples of fear people enjoy on a regular basis. But why do some people actually seek out fear? Scientists don't know for sure. Some researchers think people like the feeling of relief at the end, when we feel safe again. Others think people are really feeling excitement, not fear, when they do these things. And still others believe people actually enjoy the feeling of fear. When we seek out fear, we know we're not really in any danger. A scary movie isn't actually going to hurt you, so you can focus on the rush and excitement you feel from the fight-or-flight response, without worrying about something bad happening.

"Danger!" the hypothalamus sends out messages to the rest of your body with a chemical called adrenaline. The adrenaline messages tell your heart to beat faster; they send more sugar through your blood to your muscles; and they tell your muscles to tense up. All these fight-or-flight responses are regulated by the autonomic nervous system, and they're controlled by the hypothalamus.

The hippocampus is yet another brain structure. It stretches through the middle of your head, and it has a lot of dopamine *receptors*—neurons that are built to receive dopamine—so it plays a big role every time you feel pleasure. It also has the ability to think more rationally about the danger that your amygdala is screaming about. This is because the hippocampus is where your brain retrieves the memories it stores. Your memories help you learn from past experiences. They help you know how to respond to whatever is going.

Say a barking dog jumps out at you as you're walking along the sidewalk. Your amygdala panics: "Watch out! Scary!" Your hypothalamus kicks in, and your heart immediately starts pounding,

Text-Dependent Questions

1. Explain what neurotransmitters do—and why.

2. List three parts of the brain and explain how they are connected to emotions.

3. Explain what the "fight-or-flight response" is and how it's connected to human evolution.

4. Compare the reactions of the cortex with the reactions of the amygdala. Which of these two brain parts seems more advanced?

your muscles tense, and you breathe fast. Now your hippocampus does its job. Maybe it says, "Calm down. Remember, last time a dog barked at you like this, it turned out to be friendly." Or maybe, depending on your memories, it says, "Yup, you're right, this is a dangerous situation! The last time a dog barked at you like this, it tried to bite you. You better get out of here right now!"

Many neuroscientists think that yet another part of the brain also plays an important part in emotions—the cortex. This is where you do your *rational* thinking. It's the part of the brain that labels the feeling you're experiencing when the dog jumps out at you. It tells you, "This is fear. You're scared." Or it might say instead, "You're startled. You're surprised. That's all." It interprets not only what's going on around you but also your response to it.

Scientists are continuing their research into how emotions are experienced within the brain. Every year, they learn a little more. In the meantime, though, you can learn to understand your own emotions a little better. As you do, you'll be able to see how emotions shape your life.

Words to Understand

motivate: Encourage or give a reason to do something.
resolve: Settle or find a solution to something.

THREE

How Do Emotions Change Your Life?

Imagine if you never experienced emotion. You'd get up and go through your day without ever feeling either happiness or sadness. Nothing would scare you or upset you—but nothing would excite you or give you pleasure either. You might think it would get pretty boring—but you wouldn't even be bored, because boredom is an emotion as well. You'd have no reason to do one thing or another, because it would all be the same to you. You wouldn't care who you talked to or what you learned or what you achieved. None of it would matter to you.

Emotions are important in our lives. They're what give color and depth to our days. They're linked to all sorts of human experiences: love and friendship, creativity and artistic expression, sports and learning, business and kindness. Emotions are what *motivate* us to behave in all sorts of ways. Even for that many-times-great-grandfather of yours, emotions were still a lot more

EMOTIONAL SELF-AWARENESS

Babies start to learn about emotions by watching their mothers' faces.

Imagine if you had no emotions! Life would be pretty boring (though not as creepy as it would be if you had no face either!).

complicated than just deciding whether to fight the woolly mammoth or run away!

Emotions help us interact with each other. As very young children, we learned to read the facial expressions and actions of the people around us. We learned that when our mothers smiled, they were happy; that when our fathers laughed, something was funny; when our sisters cried, they were sad. We also learned to interpret body language and tone of voice. We understood that when our parents rose their voices, they were angry; that when our brothers jumped up and down, they were excited. Before we

Young children still lack the vocabulary to express shades of emotion. Although they may have more ways to express themselves than a newborn baby does, they will still cry when they're scared, when they're sad, when they're frustrated, and when they're angry.

Make Connections

Experts have found that outward expressions of emotions (body language) mean different things in different cultures. For example, if a young person avoids looking directly at a person in authority, it is taken as a sign of respect in some cultures—but in other cultures, this expression suggests guilt or shame. A study of Chinese and Westerners also found that Chinese people are more likely to rely on others' eyes to judge their emotions, while Westerners pay more attention to eyebrows and mouths.

even had the words to label these emotions, we were starting to understand what they meant. As we learned more words, we could use them to talk and think about feelings. We also learned how to adjust our own behaviors in response to the emotions of those around us. We remembered things that made our mothers smile, and we did those things again. We felt bad when we made someone cry (we were learning empathy), and we tried not to do the things again that hurt others.

As we get older, we become better at understanding emotions, both others' and our own. As a very young baby, crying was about the only way we could tell others we were unhappy. If we were sad or cold, lonely or angry, hungry or bored, crying was the only signal we could give to the grownups that we wanted them to do something to make our lives better. As we grew up, though, language gave us other ways to express our feelings. We learned to not only identify others' emotions but our own as well. With time and practice, we got better at knowing what we were feeling and why.

Psychologists call this skill "emotional awareness." Emotional awareness helps us know what we want and don't want. It helps

As young children, our relationships with our siblings may teach us about others' emotions, as well as our own.

As we get older, we may still struggle to get along with our siblings! But without emotions, we'd feel no connection to the people we love. They wouldn't make us angry—but they wouldn't make us laugh either.

us build relationships with others, partly because we can talk about feelings. We understand how to avoid or *resolve* conflicts better, so we get along with others more easily, without fighting and arguing. Emotions help us understand others. They help us form bonds with other people. This ability to form bonds with others is important. It's what allows us to work together on teams. It's

Research Project

Children go through various stages as they grow. Using the Internet or the library, find out the normal stages a child goes through between birth and age five. List these, and then explain how emotions relate to each stage. What role does language development play in a child's understanding of emotions?

Emotions are the "glue" that connects you and your friends.

Text-Dependent Questions

1. This chapter says that emotions motivate us to do things in life. Explain what this means.

2. How do emotions help us to interact with others?

3. Explain the process by which a baby learns about emotions.

4. What is emotional awareness?

the building block of friendship. It's the glue that holds married people together and creates families.

Some people have more emotional awareness than others. But it's a skill you can learn. As you get better at it, it will help you be more successful in life. And the more you understand how emotions interact, the more you can start to get a handle on them. Instead of letting emotions control your life, you can learn to control your emotions.

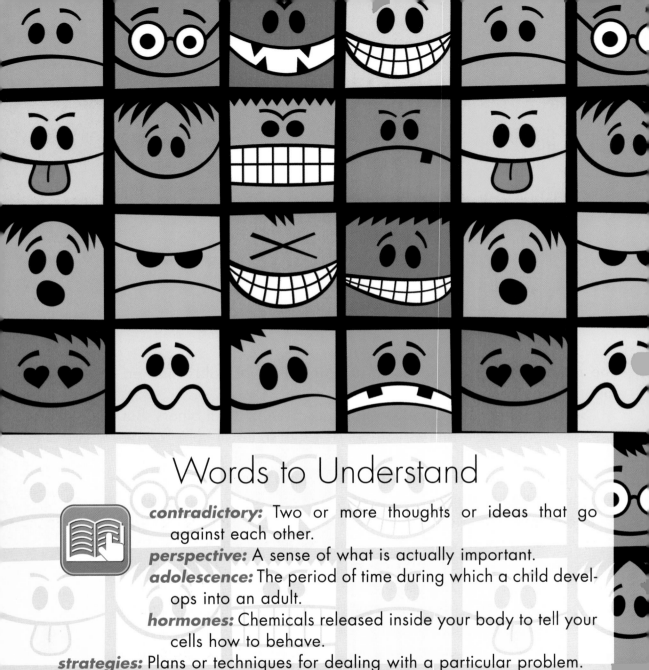

Words to Understand

contradictory: Two or more thoughts or ideas that go against each other.

perspective: A sense of what is actually important.

adolescence: The period of time during which a child develops into an adult.

hormones: Chemicals released inside your body to tell your cells how to behave.

strategies: Plans or techniques for dealing with a particular problem.

impulsive: Done without thinking about it.

compensate: Make up for something or balance something out.

constructively: Having to do with fixing or building up people or things.

realistic: Likely to actually happen.

self-control: The ability to act rationally and not give in to emotion.

interpersonal: Having to do with the interactions between people.

FOUR

UNDERSTANDING YOUR EMOTIONS

Imagine you and a friend are hanging out. You tell her about something hard that's going on in your life, and you feel a sense of comfort when you can tell she understands and cares. The two of you decide to watch a movie together, and you end up laughing and laughing. You go home thinking about how much you like your friend. The next day, though, your friend says something to you that hurts your feelings. You say something mean back to her, and before you know it, the two of you are in an argument. You feel so angry with her that you want to scream. This time when you go home, you're feeling guilty for being so mad at your friend. Same friend but entirely different emotions.

All human beings have these **contradictory** feelings. It just comes with the package of being human. Even in a single day, we go from loving our families to hating them. We wake up sad and go to bed happy. It's hard to make sense of it all. What's real? What's good and what's bad?

Feeling angry and bored is pretty normal when you're a teenager. Those feelings are caused by changes inside the adolescent brain.

Emotions are just feelings. They come and go, the same way our physical feelings—like headaches and hunger pangs and sleepiness—come and go. It's a good idea to pay attention to your feelings and be aware of them, but you should also try to keep them in *perspective*. If you're furious with your friend, it doesn't mean you're a bad person. Emotions aren't bad or good; they're just feelings, the same way headaches and hunger and sleepiness are feelings.

BAD MOODS AND BEING AN ADOLESCENT

Do you ever find yourself feeling grumpy and out of sorts, even though you have no good reason to be angry? Or do you wake up feeling sad some days for no real reason? Everyone experiences these feelings sometimes, and emotional ups-and-downs are even more common during *adolescence*. Not only do you have *hormones* surging through your body, getting you ready to be sexually mature, but lots of other things are going on inside your body as well.

Researchers have looked inside the teenage brain and discovered that adolescent brains really are different from adult brains. Your prefrontal cortex—the part of your brain responsible for things like organizing plans and ideas, coming up with *strategies*, and controlling impulses—won't be fully developed until you're in your late twenties.

Meanwhile, your dopamine levels aren't at the level they will be when you're an adult. Dopamine is the chemical messenger that gives us pleasure, but it also allows us to figure out what to pay attention to and what is background noise. Without the right amount of dopamine, it's hard to sort through our emotions. *Everything* can seem like a big deal!

As a teenager, you also need more sleep than you will when you're an adult. You probably already know that you like to stay up late and sleep late—but you may not have known that your body is built that way. Teenagers' sleep cycles are different from children's and adults'. Unfortunately, life doesn't

Getting enough sleep is an important step toward managing your emotions.

always accommodate this difference. If every day was a Saturday, you'd be all set—but instead, you're probably expected to be up and awake early every school day, even though you were up until midnight the night before. This means that you may not be getting enough sleep. But your brain *needs* sleep. Brain chemicals aren't produced the same way when you're not getting the sleep you need. Emotions are harder to manage where you're tired.

Scientists have also found that when it comes to adolescents identifying their own and others' emotions, they aren't as good at it as most adults are. Also, teens and adults used different areas of the brain to process their feelings. Teens rely much more on the amygdala, while adults rely more on the frontal cortex. Your amygdala is more **impulsive** (remember, it's fond of shouting, "Danger! Danger!"—and it may also shout things like, "Wow! Let's do that right *now*!"), while your frontal cortex is the part of your brain that thinks things through. It's the part that makes judgments based on reason. It can stop to think about the consequences of your actions.

So it's not your fault if you're struggling to handle your emotions. It doesn't mean you're a bad person. All the adults on the planet lived through the same thing back when they were adolescents. Doing your best to get enough sleep is one thing that will help, but while you're waiting for your brain to mature, there are other things you can do that will help you to better manage your emotions.

MANAGING YOUR EMOTIONS

Like headaches and hunger and sleepiness, your feelings, both positive and negative, tell you to pay attention because you need to do something. Maybe you need to try to relax or eat a sandwich or go to bed—or maybe you need to take some other action.

When it comes to emotions, it's what you *do* that is more important than what you *feel*. If you get so angry at your sister that you say or do hurtful things, there will be consequences to your

Talking honestly with a good friend helps you be more aware of your emotions.

actions. If you choose to talk about your anger, though, and try to compromise and find a solution, there will be different consequences. Learning how to express emotions in acceptable ways is an important part of managing your emotions.

All emotions tell you something about yourself and your situation. Sometimes, though, you might not want to hear the message your emotions are sending you. For example, maybe you notice yourself feeling jealous every time your best friend gets a good grade. You don't want to feel jealous of her, though, because friends are supposed to be happy for each other, so you try to ignore your feeling. Every time it pops up, you push it out of your head. You pretend to yourself that it was never there at all.

But ignoring bad feelings or pretending they don't exist isn't usually a very good way to manage your emotions. Your jealousy of your friend will probably continue to shape the way you act with her, no matter how much you try to pretend it doesn't. In fact, the more you try not to think about your jealousy, the stronger it may grow.

Make Connections

Emotions like anger and fear come from your amygdala. Scientists say that this is the most primitive, least evolved part of the human brain. Some psychiatrists and neurologists refer to this as the "reptilian brain." This is because reptiles rely on a similar structure to control their instinctive behaviors, which include aggression, mating, catching prey, and dominating rivals. You don't really want to go through life functioning with the same skills a reptile has! Crocodiles, for example, aren't known for their ability to form strong bonds with other crocodiles, and you've probably never met a lizard that was warm and loving. You want to give your higher brain a chance to exercise its far more sophisticated skills, which will help you build and maintain the relationships that are important to you.

Psychologists say it's better to notice our emotional reactions and label them honestly. Feeling them doesn't make us bad people. When we're honest with ourselves about our emotions, we can handle them better. We don't have to think about them constantly. A lot of the time, we don't have to even talk about them. If we do decide to talk about them, we can decide how we do that, instead of letting them influence our behavior indirectly.

With your friend, for example, if you try to ignore your feelings of jealousy, you may find that you're snapping at her and saying things that aren't very kind. She doesn't understand what's going on, and she's hurt. But if you face your feelings, you might then say to her, "I'm really sorry. I guess I was just feeling jealous of you because you always seem to get better grades than me." If the two of you talk about your feelings openly, calmly, and kindly, you may discover that she's jealous of you too, but for other reasons. You feel better about yourself now. Maybe the two of you

Stress is the feeling you get when life comes at you too fast. It can be hard to handle life's ordinary emotions when you have more stress than usual in your life.

Make Connections

Everyone has up days and down days. Some things in life are hard to deal with, emotionally. But if you feel out of sorts day after day, it could be a sign of depression. Depression is a psychological disorder that keeps a person from living life normally. It isn't only a sad feeling. It can also include feelings of boredom, hopelessness, anger, impatience, and just general moodiness. These negative emotions get in the way of enjoying life. They interfere with relationships. If you notice yourself experiencing something like this, talk to a counselor or doctor. They'll be able to help you find ways to get over your depression.

can laugh about how silly you've both been. You'll come away with your friendship stronger. With time, your negative feelings fade away.

EMOTIONS AND STRESS

People who don't know how to handle their emotions often experience a great deal of stress. When we talk about "stress," we're referring to the feeling we get when we wonder whether we can cope with all the things life is asking us to handle. Anything that poses a challenge to our well-being can cause us stress—and even good things (getting a new pet, starting a new job, moving to a new home, or going to college, for example) can cause stress as well.

Stress is an emotional reaction that was meant to prepare humans for danger. It's connected to the fight-or-flight response. It causes these physical reactions:

- Blood pressure rises.
- Breathing becomes more rapid.

- Digestive system slows down.
- Heart rate (pulse) rises.
- Immune system doesn't work as well, since the body's energy is getting ready for other dangers.
- Muscles become tense. (They're getting ready to go into action.)
- People may not be able to sleep. (The body is in a state of extra alertness.)

All these physical responses are hard on the body. Your body can't really tell the difference between stress that's caused by a fight with your best friend, the stress that's caused by getting ready to go away to college, and the stress that's caused by a death in your family. From your body's perspective, it's all the same. When people have too much stress, they are more likely to get sick. But there are things you can do to manage stress.

Start by identifying what's causing you stress. It may surprise you (because sometimes even good things, like a new boyfriend or a new job, can be causing you stress). Talking with someone you trust can help you understand your own feelings better. Writing in a journal also helps. Once you know what's causing your feelings, you don't have to dwell on it—but you'll understand yourself and your reactions better. You'll be able to take action to *compensate* for the stress.

One of these actions might be talking even more often with someone you trust, a friend, a teacher, a family member, or a counselor. Make sure it's someone who can understand what you're going through. Talking about your emotions will help them not feel so stressful. Don't be afraid to ask for help. Together, you may also be able to come up with new ideas for dealing with the situation better.

Physical exercise also helps us manage our emotions. Going for a walk or playing a game of basketball will release some of the physical effects of emotional stress. Exercise also makes our brains release chemicals that produce feelings of well-being.

Make time to relax and get enough sleep. No matter how busy you are, your body needs time to rest. Being tired affects how your brain works. You're more likely to feel grouchy or sad if you haven't had enough sleep.

Be careful what you eat. Stress can affect appetite. Some people may not feel like eating at all when they're stressed, while other people might overeat. What's most important is that you get good nutrition. Proper nutrition will help your immune system fight off germs, so you're not as likely to get sick when you're stressed. Good nutrition can also lift your mood and increase your energy level. Be sure to eat plenty of fruits and vegetables, and don't skip meals!

Express yourself creatively. Sing, dance, draw pictures, write a poem. Creativity helps us handle our emotions positively and *constructively*.

Look on the bright side. Find reason to laugh. Notice the good things in life. Focus on your strengths. Be extra kind to yourself. Whether it's going for a walk, listening to your favorite music, or hanging out with someone who always makes you laugh, make sure you do whatever it takes to give yourself a break from the stress. You'll be able to cope with it better.

And last, be *realistic* about what you can handle. Sometimes we take on more than our emotions can deal with at once. If you're taking an extra hard math course, this might not be a good time to get an after-school job. If someone in your family just died, you may want to take an easier course load while you're dealing with your grief. Give your emotions time to heal. Be patient with yourself. Don't expect more of yourself than your emotions can handle.

Stress is normal. It's a part of our emotional lives. By being more aware of it, we can allow it to point out something in our lives that needs attention. It might remind us that we need to slow down or focus more. Once we find a way to solve the problem, the pressure and stress will ease.

The more you deal with the stress that goes hand-in-hand with emotions, the better you'll get at managing your emotions. Like

No two people's emotional reactions are exactly alike. One of these people may be thrilled and elated—and the other one may be so terrified he's peeing his pants!

anything else in life, it gets easier with practice. Remember when you learned something that seemed hard at first. Maybe it was riding a bike. If you think back, when you first got on a bicycle, you probably felt as though you were never going to be able to pedal down the street the way the older kids could. But little by little, the more you practiced, the better you got at it, and the more your confidence grew. Eventually, you could keep your bike balanced and controlled.

And you can do the same things with your emotions. Here are some things to keep in mind:

- **_Your emotions will not be exactly like anyone else's._** Psychologists say that emotions are "subjective," which means that each person experiences emotions from an individual point of view. Different people may experience different emotions even though they're being faced with exactly the same situation. Imagine, for example, that you're about to jump out of an airplane for your very first skydiving adventure. Maybe you feel absolute terror. But the person next to you is smiling from ear to ear; she's so excited and happy that she can hardly wait to leap. Meanwhile, both of you may be experiencing similar body responses: both of your hearts are pounding and you're both breathing quickly. Adrenaline is surging through both your bodies. But you label those feelings as terror, and she labels them as excitement. Those different reactions don't make either of you a better person than the other. Instead, they have to do with the other points on this list.

- **_Emotions can be learned._** In the example we just gave, the woman who is so thrilled to be jumping out of an airplane may have learned to enjoy the shot of adrenaline she gets from danger. Her reaction and yours may be different because you have different upbringings. Your past experiences are different. However, you could learn

Is this young man terrified—or thrilled? Some emotions can be very close together. Whether we give them negative or positive labels can depend on our point of view.

to be more like her. The more times you jump out of that airplane—or engage in other high-adrenaline sports—the more likely you are to feel comfortable with the feeling. You may no longer label the feeling you get as "terror." You may start to find the feeling exciting.

- **Our emotions are shaped by those around us.** Have you ever seen a little kid fall down and then look up quickly to see how his parents are reacting? If his parents smile and act as though everything is okay, the child may scramble to his feet and run happily on his way. But if, instead, he sees fear or pain on his parents' faces, he may burst into tears. Or imagine you're back on that plane, getting ready to jump, but this time you're standing next to someone who is more terrified than you are. His emotions are likely to make yours even worse.

- **Our emotions are partly shaped by our emotional makeup.** Some people tend to be more fearful than others. Some people experience more intense emotions than others. Some people have a gloomy outlook on life, while others are little rays of sunshine. Emotional makeup is shaped by a variety of things—our genes, our upbringing, and our life experiences—but once it's in place, it will influence our emotional lives. Happy people feel happiness more easily; grouchy people get irritated more quickly. But keep in mind the point listed above: emotions can also be learned!

The more you make a habit of paying attention to your emotions—noticing them and labeling them honestly—the more you'll be able to manage them in ways that help you get along better in life. Eventually, this habit becomes an automatic skill you'll have as you live your life. Psychologists sometimes call this skill "emotional intelligence."

Research Project

Use the Internet and the library to find out more about stress and the fight-or-flight response. Make a poster of the human body and label and highlight the parts of the body that are affected by stress. Include on your poster an explanation of why each these reactions are helpful—and why each can also be hard on your body.

EMOTIONAL INTELLIGENCE

Your emotional intelligence has to do with your ability to pay attention to your own and other people's emotions—and then use this information to act wisely in relationships. Experts say that emotional intelligence has five parts:

1. Self-awareness: recognizing your feelings.
2. Managing emotions: finding appropriate ways to handle your emotions in various situations.
3. Motivation: using *self-control* to channel your emotions toward a goal
4. Empathy: understanding the emotional perspectives of other people
5. Handling relationships: using your understanding of emotions to handle social relationships and to develop *interpersonal* skills.

Researchers are beginning to develop tests that can measure emotional intelligence. Scientists who study emotions generally believe that people with high emotional intelligence usually work well on teams. They also make good leaders. People with low emotional intelligence, though, often get emotional signals wrong. As a result, they have difficulty with relationships. Scientists believe

Text-Dependent Questions

1. List two ways that teenage brains are different from adult brains—and explain how this can affect teenagers' behavior.

2. Explain the connection between sleep and emotions.

3. Why do scientists sometimes refer to the amygdala as your "lizard brain"?

4. List seven physical reactions to stress.

5. What are five ways to handle stress better?

6. Explain the five parts of emotional intelligence.

that many factors go into emotional intelligence, including your genes and your upbringing—but they also agree that people can learn to become more emotionally intelligent.

Emotions are important. The more you understand what they are and how they work, the more you'll be able to use them to help you manage your entire life better. The first step is simple: pay attention to your feelings. Pay attention to others' feelings as well. Emotions, even negative ones, contain all sort of information—and learning to be more emotionally intelligent will improve your life.

Find Out More

IN BOOKS

Lamia, Mary. *Emotions! Making Sense of Your Feelings*. Washington, D.C.: Magination Press, 2012.

Madison, Lynda. *The Feelings Book: The Care and Keeping of Your Emotions*. Middletown, Wisc.: American Girl Press, 2002.

McClaren, Carla. *The Language of Emotions: What Your Feelings Are Trying to Tell You*. Louisville, Colo: Sounds True, 2010.

ONLINE

The Complete Guide to Understanding Your Emotions
www.psychologytoday.com/blog/fulfillment-any-age/201205/the-complete-guide-understanding-your-emotions

Developing Emotional Awareness
www.helpguide.org/toolkit/developing_emotional_awareness.htm

Understanding Emotions
www.trans4mind.com/heart/emotions.html

Understanding Emotions Without Words
www.sciencedaily.com/releases/2011/11/111102093045.htm

Understanding Your Emotions
www.wire.wisc.edu/yourself/Emotions/Understanding_emotions.aspx

Series Glossary of Key Terms

adrenaline: An important body chemical that helps prepare your body for danger. Too much adrenaline can also cause stress and anxiety.

amygdala: An almond-shaped area within the brain where the flight-or-flight response takes place.

autonomic nervous system: The part of your nervous system that works without your conscious control, regulating body functions such as heartbeat, breathing, and digestion.

cognitive: Having to do with thinking and conscious mental activities.

cortex: The area of your brain where rational thinking takes place.

dopamine: A brain chemical that gives pleasure as a reward for certain activities.

endorphins: Brain chemicals that create feelings of happiness.

fight-or-flight response: Your brain's reaction to danger, which sends out messages to the rest of the body, getting it ready to either run away or fight.

hippocampus: Part of the brain's limbic system that plays an important role in memory.

hypothalamus: The brain structure that gets messages out to your body's autonomic nervous system, preparing it to face danger.

limbic system: The part of the brain where emotions are processed.

neurons: Nerve cells found in the brain, spinal cord, and throughout the body.

neurotransmitters: Chemicals that carry messages across the tiny gaps between nerve cells.

serotonin: A neurotransmitter that plays a role in happiness and depression.

stress: This feeling that life is just too much to handle can be triggered by anything that poses a threat to our well-being, including emotions, external events, and physical illnesses.

Index

adolescence 42, 44–45, 47
adrenaline 30, 55, 57
amygdala 29–31, 47, 49, 59
antidepressants 25
anxiety 25, 27
autonomic nervous system 30

brain 8, 13, 15–21, 24–25,
    27–31, 44–45, 47, 49,
    52–53, 59

cognitive appraisal theory 15,
    19
cortex 29, 31, 45, 47
culture 37
counselor 51–52

Darwin, Charles 14–15, 18–19
depression 25, 27, 51
dopamine 27, 30, 45

emotional awareness 37, 41
emotional intelligence 57–59
empathy 8, 13, 37, 58
evolution 14, 18, 31

fight-or-flight response 29–31,
    51, 58

frontal lobe 29

happiness 11, 15, 21, 23, 29,
    33, 57
heart 11, 13, 15, 17, 23, 29–
    30, 52, 55
hippocampus 30–31
hormones 17, 42, 45
hypothalamus 29–30

limbic system 29
love 13, 15, 23, 33, 39

MRI 16–18, 21

neurologist 8, 17, 49
neurons 25–27, 30
neurotransmitters 25–27, 31
norepinephrine 25, 27

optimism 8, 18

psychologist 8, 13, 15, 17, 25,
    37, 49, 55, 57

sadness 11, 13, 23, 29, 33
serotonin 25, 27
stress 27, 50–53, 58–59

Picture Credits

About the Author & Consultant

Rosa Waters lives in New York State. She has worked as a writer for several years, producing works on health, history, and other topics.

Cindy Croft is director of the Center for Inclusive Child Care at Concordia University, St. Paul, Minnesota where she also serves as faculty in the College of Education. She is field faculty at the University of Minnesota Center for Early Education and Development program and teaches for the Minnesota on-line Eager To Learn program. She has her M.A. in education with early childhood emphasis. She has authored *The Six Keys: Strategies for Promoting Children's Mental Health in Early Childhood Programs* and co-authored *Children and Challenging Behavior: Making Inclusion Work* with Deborah Hewitt. She has worked in the early childhood field for the past twenty years.

BOOK CHARGING CARD

Accession No. _____ Call No. _____

Author _____

Title _____

Borrower's Name	Date